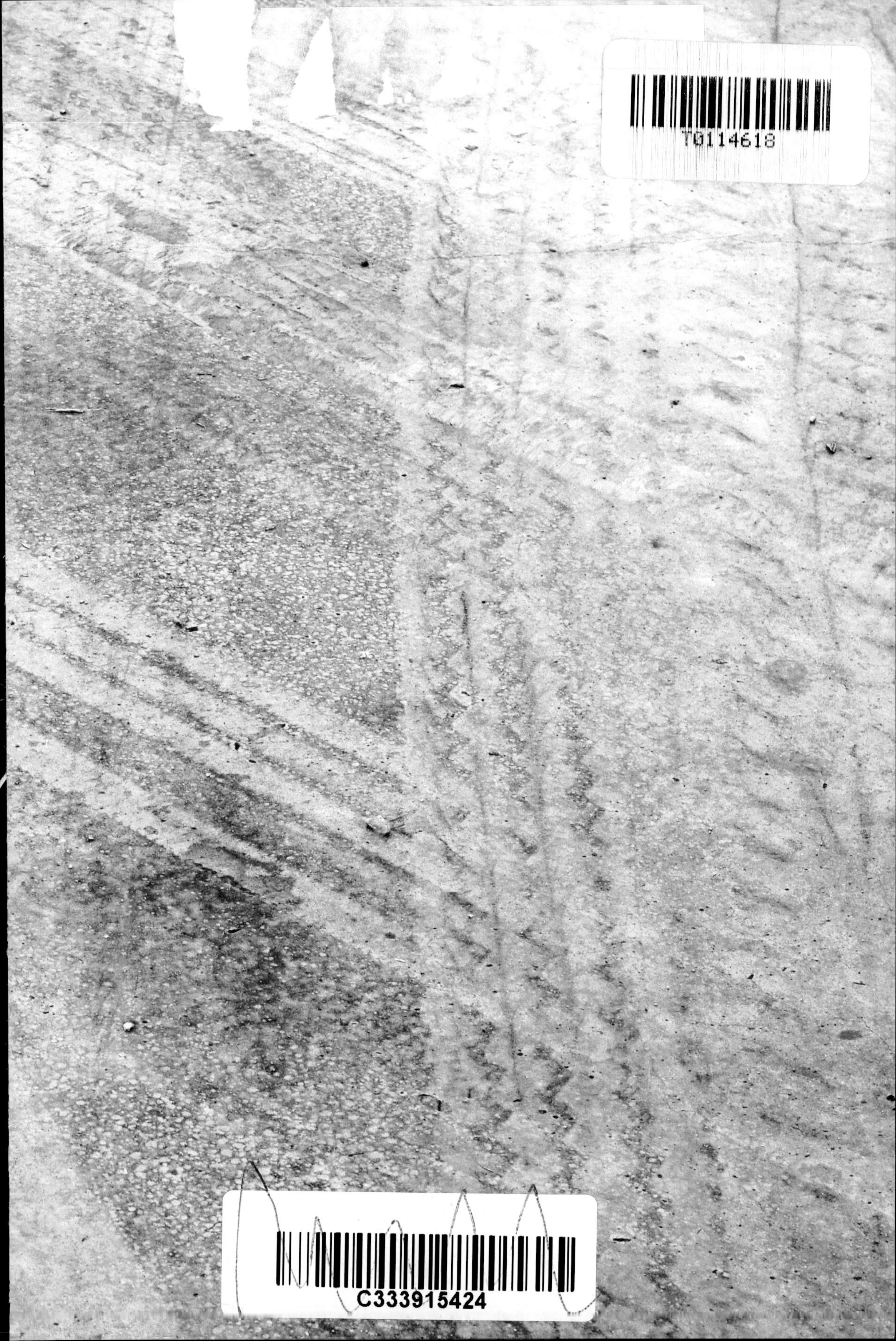

The Inside Track

MOTO GP RIDER

Paul Mason

FRANKLIN WATTS
EDGE

LONDON·SYDNEY

Franklin Watts
First published in Great Britain in 2016 by
The Watts Publishing Group

Copyright © The Watts Publishing
Group 2016

Credits
Executive editor: Adrian Cole
Series designer: Mayer Media
Design manager: Peter Scoulding
Picture researcher: Diana Morris

Photo acknowledgements:
The Age/Getty Images: 30cr. efecreata mediagroup/
Shutterstock: 28. Ivan Garcia/Shutterstock: 19b,
20c. Rodrigo Garrido/Shutterstock: 30tr. Getty
Images: 16t, 22t. Gleb Stock/Shutterstock: 6tl.
Rainer Herhaus/Shutterstock: front cover t & c, 1, 4t,
5t, 6b, 10b, 11t, 13c, 14c, 17t, 18b, 21c, 26, 29t,
29b, 30crb. hxdbzxy/Shutterstock: 5b. Karim Jaafar/
AFP/Getty Images: 7t. JRH/Shutterstock: 23b, 24b.
Evren Kalinbacak/Shutterstock: 4b. kts design/
Shutterstock: 4tl. Mirco Lazzari/Getty Images: 30cra.
MaxiSport/Shutterstock: 15c. Simon Miles/Getty
Images: 30br. Christian Pondella /Getty Images:
8c, 17b, 27. Gines Romero/Shutterstock: 12l, 25.
wikimedia commons: 31tl, 31cr, 31cl, 31br.

Dewey number 796.7'5'0922
HB ISBN 978 1 4451 4699 7
Library ebook ISBN 978 1 4451 4701 7

Printed in China

Franklin Watts
An imprint of
Hachette Children's Group
Part of The Watts Publishing Group
Carmelite House
50 Victoria Embankment
London EC4Y 0DZ

An Hachette UK Company
www.hachette.co.uk

www.franklinwatts.co.uk

*The narrative within this book is a work
of fiction and all statements purporting
to be facts are not necessarily true.*

*The statistics were correct at the time this book
was printed, but because of the nature of the sport,
it cannot be guaranteed that they are now accurate.*

*The tweets in this book have been reproduced as
they originally appeared on Twitter, and as a result
may contain inaccuracies and do not express the
views or opinions of the Publisher or Author.*

CONTENTS

RIDER BIO

NAME:	Marc Marquez
RACE NUMBER:	93
BORN:	1993
COUNTRY:	Spain

Aggressive and super-talented, Marquez brought a whole new riding style to MotoGP when he started his first season in 2013.

In 2013, Marc Marquez hit the MotoGP scene like a bomb going off. It was his rookie season in MotoGP — and it was like no rookie season anyone had seen before.

By the final race of 2013, Marquez had become...

◉ the youngest-ever top-class World Champion

◉ the first rookie title winner for 35 years

◉ the youngest-ever pole-sitter and race winner

In 2014 Marquez was again red hot. He won the first ten races of the season. By round 15, with three races still to go, he was World Champion for a second time. Many people thought it was inevitable that Marquez would be champion again in 2015. In fact, he was so nearly unbeatable that people began to make comparisons with the greatest motorbike racer ever: "The Doctor", Valentino Rossi.

VALENTINO ROSSI: "THE DOCTOR"

RIDER BIO

NAME: Valentino Rossi

RACE NUMBER: 46

BORN: 1979

COUNTRY: Italy

Rossi went into the 2015 season riding for Yamaha — the team with which he had won World Championships in 2004, 2005, 2008, 2009 and 2010.

In Italian, *Dottore* (Doctor) is a title for people who are really good at something. Valentino Rossi is one of the best bike racers of all time.

At the start of the 2015 season, Rossi was:

◉ winner of 69 MotoGP races

◉ winner of nine World Championships

◉ the only rider in history to have won the 125cc, 250cc, 500cc and MotoGP World Championships

In 2015, though, Rossi was 36 — ancient in bike-racing terms. He had only won five races in the last five years. People started to ask themselves: is The Doctor past it? The year before, Rossi had started working with a new crew chief, Silvano Galbusera. His riding style changed. The changes brought results: Rossi won two races, and came second to Marquez in the World Championship. The question was, could The Doctor challenge for one more World Championship in 2015 — six years after he had won his last one?*

*The winner of the 2015 season is revealed on page 32.

crew chief engineer in charge of preparing the bike for racing

> This is the story of Marc's battle with Rossi — told from the inside!

The battle for the 2015 MotoGP World Championship began on 29 March, at the Losail Circuit in Qatar. The Repsol Honda team was confident that Marc would win — but the result was a horrible shock.

In 2014, Marc won this race, with Rossi a split second behind — right on his exhaust pipe. In 2015, though, Marc got a terrible start. As other riders roared away, he was forced off the track. He had to rejoin right at the back.

Marc fought his way back through the field brilliantly. But all the hard braking, accelerating and cornering he had to do wore out his tyres. In the end, the best he could finish was fifth place. Marc tried to put a brave face on it:

@marcmarquez93
It's a shame my mistake, but we finished the race :) We were all gutted, though – especially as Rossi rode unbelievably well.

↩ ↻ 5 ★ 6 •••

QATAR MOTOGP FINAL RESULTS

1	Valentino **Rossi**	Honda	25
2	Andrea **Dovizioso**	Ducati	20
3	Andrea **Iannone**	Ducati	16
4	Jorge **Lorenzo**	Yamaha	13
5	Marc **Marquez**	Honda	11

Rossi, meanwhile, had been in tenth place at the end of the first lap — but then we watched him overtake rider after rider. With four laps to go, Rossi was in second. The commentators got very excited:

"What is [Rossi] made of? 36 years old, nine-times World Champion... The Italian is nothing short of a god."

Then, with little more than a lap to go, Rossi took the lead. He won! We realised then that The Doctor was back — we were in for a real battle this year. The result in Qatar made the second race of the season, this weekend in Texas, feel like a must-win event!

season the time from the first race in a championship until the last one

AT THE CIRCUIT
OF THE AMERICAS

DATE: Friday 10 April 2015
PLACE: Austin, Texas

It's great to be back in the USA! Marc won his first-ever MotoGP here in Austin in 2013. He loves it here — which is good. We need to get his season back on track.

Every once in a while Marc's fans get a nice surprise from him. Yesterday he sent out this message:

@marcmarquez93
I just left 2 Austin @MotoGP Paddock passes at the Barton Creek Square @Oakley Store. First person to get there and say 'IAM93' gets them

↰ ⇄ 12 ★ 8 ...

Apparently the Barton Creek Square store was mobbed!

Meanwhile, back at the track the bikes have been unpacked, built up and then checked by the scrutineers. The scrutineering wasn't as serious as in Qatar, where they looked at *everything*. Here they just checked any changes we'd made to the bike. It's still a bit nerve-wracking waiting to get the OK, though.

scrutineers officials who check the bikes are legal to race

Austin locals have a slogan, "Keep Austin Weird"! The first free-practice session (FP1) definitely lives up to that...

First, it's raining like crazy...

Then some of the marshals go (temporarily) missing...

Then the riders have to stop because there is a stray dog on the track!

Fortunately, things get less weird for FP2. Marc goes faster than in FP1 by 15 seconds. Everyone else is faster too, of course ... but at the end of the day, it is Marc at the top of the time sheets.

FREE PRACTICE 2
2015 GRAND PRIX OF THE AMERICAS

P	RIDER	COUNTRY	TEAM	TIME
1	Marc **Marquez**	Spain	Repsol Honda	2.04.835
2	Cal **Crutchlow**	UK	CWM LCR Honda	+0.327
3	Andrea **Iannone**	Italy	Ducati	+0.028
4	Aleix **Espargaro**	Spain	Suzuki Ecstar	+0.374
5	Andrea **Dovizioso**	Italy	Ducati	+0.082

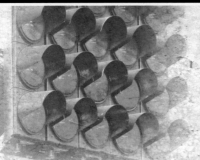

marshals people around the track in charge of safety

DATE: Saturday 11 April 2015

These last two free practice sessions are where things get serious! Before, teams were experimenting a bit with the engine, suspension and tyres. Now, the riders need to go quick.

There's one cloud on the horizon. Our weather forecasters think it might rain again today. Rain could upset our plans. We've made all kinds of calculations about track-surface temperatures, tyres and suspension — but if it rains, everything changes.

 @marcmarquez93
Really looking forward to riding this afternoon at #AmericasGP

RIDER BIO

NAME:	Jorge Lorenzo
RACE NUMBER:	99
BORN:	1987
COUNTRY:	Spain

MotoGP World Champion in 2010 and 2012* (when he was either first or second in every race he finished), Lorenzo is known for his stylish riding.

*The winner of the 2015 season is revealed on page 32.

track-surface temperature temperature of the track surface, which affects how hot and grippy tyres are

FP3: fortunately, the rain doesn't arrive. Marc is fastest again. Behind him is Cal Crutchlow on a satellite Honda, then the Yamahas of Lorenzo and Rossi. They look worryingly quick: this shouldn't be a track that suits Yamaha, but they're only 0.345 seconds behind.

FP4: the good news is that Marc finishes fastest, and Rossi drops back a bit. In fact, he's nearly a second slower. Is Rossi feeling the pressure? We're hoping so — but as this is his 222nd MotoGP race, it's unlikely! The reward for the ten fastest riders in free practice is that they don't have to ride in qualifying race 1 (Q1). The riders and crews are tired, so a break from trying to do fast laps is welcome. In the garage, of course, it's still crazy-busy working on the bikes and analysing data!

FREE PRACTICE 4
2015 GRAND PRIX OF THE AMERICAS

P	RIDER	COUNTRY	TEAM	TIME
1	Marc **Marquez**	Spain	Repsol Honda	2.03.548
2	Jorge **Lorenzo**	Italy	Movistar Yamaha	+0.355
3	Andrea **Dovizioso**	Italy	Ducati	+0.352
4	Valentino **Rossi**	Italy	Movistar Yamaha	+0.087
5	Andrea **Iannone**	Italy	Ducati	+0.024

QP1 AND QP2

Qualifying starts, like always, with the fastest ten riders sitting out the first session. Marc tries to relax, but it's tricky: there's a lot going on, and he knows the 15 minutes of Q2 can make or break his race weekend.

Setting one of the top three times will mean Marc starts on the front row of the grid. From there, it's easier to get to the first corner. And if that happens, he'll try to stretch ahead quickly, then ride steadily, unless someone starts to catch him up.

Q2 is always exciting — this is the shootout for pole, after all — and Marc doesn't disappoint. With just three minutes left, he is only seventh fastest — but on a fast lap. Then, disaster! A warning light flashes up on the dashboard of his bike!

shootout for pole the final battle for pole position (first on the starting grid)
grid the lines that mark the starting places on a racetrack

Marc stops at the side of the track, leaps over the pit wall, and sprints down the pit lane in full leathers and helmet. His pit crew has seen what is happening, so his spare bike is out of the garage with the engine running.

Marc leaps on, heads out on track, and sets the fastest time of the session — despite nearly crashing at turn 10. And he isn't just fastest ... he smashes the lap record!

You've got to love this tweet:

@marcmarquez93
Pole al sprint! hahaha

FINAL QUALIFYING
2015 GRAND PRIX OF THE AMERICAS

P	RIDER	COUNTRY	TEAM	TIME
1	Marc **Marquez**	Spain	Repsol Honda	2.02.135
2	Andrea **Dovizioso**	Italy	Ducati	+0.339
3	Jorge **Lorenzo**	Italy	Movistar Yamaha	+0.066
4	Valentino **Rossi**	Italy	Movistar Yamaha	+0.033
5	Cal **Crutchlow**	UK	CWM LCR Honda	+0.040

Race day! Even though Marc's been racing since he was a tiny kid, he still gets excited before a race. (So does everyone on the team, actually...)

The riders all have their own way of preparing for a race. Rossi's is very complicated. He watches the start of the Moto3 race, to see how long it takes the start lights to go out. He always puts his boots and gloves on in a particular order. And then before actually riding the bike, Rossi says he has a set routine:

1. Stop about 2 m away and reach down to my boots

2. Crouch down beside the bike and hold on to the right-side footpeg: *"It's just a moment to focus and 'talk' to my bike."*

3. Get on from the same side

4. Stand up while riding off down the pit lane

Moto3 race for 250cc bikes, which is held before a MotoGP race

Marc doesn't have a routine like Rossi's — not many do! He just tries to relax, which means he has to be kept him away from his phone. There's an online motocross game that Marc and Dani Pedrosa both play. Dani's almost always faster at it, and when Marc sees the times online he gets really annoyed!

RIDER BIO

NAME:	Dani Pedrosa
RACE NUMBER:	85
BORN:	1985
COUNTRY:	Spain

Second in the MotoGP World Championship in 2007, 2010 and 2012, but Pedrosa has struggled with injuries in every season. Without them, he might have become World Champion.

In the garage, the discussion is about which tyres will work best in the race. A medium front tyre is softer. It has more grip, so you can set fast lap times — but the tyre will wear out at the end of the race. A hard front will be slower at the beginning, but will last longer.

Marc has decided a hard front tyre will be best. It looks like Rossi has made the same decision.

LIGHTS OUT AND GO!

The riders are on the grid, ready to race. They crouch over their bikes, waiting for the start lights to come on. After all the work, this is it: 21 laps that will decide the winner.

Next to Marc on the front row are Andrea Dovizioso and Lorenzo. On the row behind are Rossi, Cal Crutchlow and Scott Redding.

One start light comes on. The riders rev their engines, and the noise is deafening. A second light comes on, then a third, fourth, fifth. There's a pause ... then all the lights go out, and the bikes leap forward like hunting cats.

Dovizioso's powerful Ducati blasts him into the lead at the first corner. Marc slots in behind, then Rossi squeezes into third. Marc could have had a better start — but it could be worse. At this moment in the last race, he was in last place!

rev turn the throttle so that the engine generates lots of power

From the fourth row of the grid, Bradley Smith got a monster start. He's now in fourth place! Smith is riding a satellite Yamaha — but he's still managed to get in front of Lorenzo, who's on a factory bike.

RIDER BIO

Name:	Bradley Smith
Race number:	38
Born:	1990
Country:	UK

A Tech3 Yamaha rider since 2011, Smith moved into their MotoGP team in 2013. In 2014 he came third at the Australian Grand Prix — a great achievement for a rider from a satellite team.

Behind the lead riders it's mayhem. Scott Redding got a terrible start, then tried to make up the lost places too quickly. Midway through the lap he skidded and lost control. He took out another rider as he crashed. Somehow, the rest of the racers avoided the accident. Everyone continued with the race.

factory bike a bike from one of the main manufacturer teams
took out crashed into and knocked over

A NEW LEADER

Last year, Marc led every single lap of the race here in Austin. This year, though, it's Dovizioso who finishes the first lap in first place.

Even though Marc is in second, no one panics. We've seen that Dovizioso is using a medium front tyre. It's more grippy than the hard tyre Marc is using, so Dovizioso can brake and corner better. But we know the medium tyre will wear out more quickly — and when that happens, Marc will overtake!

We're more worried about what Rossi might do. He's using the same tyres as Marc — and looking very fast. With 19 laps to go, the commentator says:

"Valentino Rossi is looking menacing. He's all over the back of Marc Marquez."

RIDER BIO

Name:	Andrea Dovizioso
Race number:	4
Born:	1986
Country:	Italy

Dovizioso (nickname: Dovi) joined Ducati in 2013. By 2015, he had helped them develop a bike good enough to challenge for the MotoGP World Championship.

LAP 3 If Rossi was any closer to the back of Marc's bike, he'd be able to jump on! Even for us in the Honda garage, this is exciting racing.

Race commentary: "That's what we want to see: the two top dogs in the world racing each other."

All of Rossi's tricks and techniques are on show: he sticks out his foot coming into turns; he takes an unusual line through corners; he looks like he's about to attack, then pulls back. He's trying to unsettle Marc and force him to make a mistake.

Marc, though, keeps his head down and just looks tidy — which we're happy to see. It probably means he could still go a bit faster. When Marc is really charging, he often looks as though he's about to crash!

line path taken around a bend in a racetrack
tidy keeping a good body shape and track position

With 17 laps to go, Marc starts to look more like he's really pushing his speed. We're seeing the riding style he's famous for.

Marc likes moving about on the bike, putting his body at unusual angles. For years before he appeared, riders had been hanging off their bikes and putting their knee on the track while cornering. Until Marc, though, no one had put their elbow down! Now they're all doing it.

Marc's team-mate Dani Pedrosa once said that:

"It seems like he's [about to crash] all the time, but he's not crashing."

As soon as he increases his speed, Marc slides past Dovizioso. This is perfect tactics for us at Honda. Marc now has Dovizioso acting as a barrier between himself and Rossi. He needs to pull ahead while Rossi is stuck there.

elbow down dragging your elbow on the track while cornering

LAP 5   Rossi is clearly being held up by Dovizioso, but he just can't get past. Last year, Rossi's speed dropped badly at the end of this race as his front tyre wore out. Maybe he's having the same problem this time?

Race commentary:
"Valentino is desperate to get past Dovi."

LAP 6   Then, with 15 laps to go, Marc does his fastest lap of the whole race so far. It's starting to become obvious that during the first part of the race, when he seemed a bit slower, he was really just saving the tyres.

Race commentary: "Slowly but surely, Marc Marquez is easing away now."

Further back, Rossi finally passes Dovizioso — but the more powerful Ducati blasts straight back past. Then the same thing happens again! While this ding-dong battle is slowing them down, other riders are catching up behind — and Marc is pulling away in front!

saving the tyres riding less aggressively, so that your tyres stay grippy for longer

LAP 7

14 laps to go, Rossi finally gets past Dovizioso for a couple of turns. Can he stay there? Can he catch up to Marc? It's game on!

First Rossi has to stay in front of Dovizioso. In the garage, we can see from the slow-motion shots on TV that Dovizioso's tyres are cooked. Are Rossi's any better?

They must be, because Rossi stays in front for several bends. He's trying to pull out a lead of a second or two. Otherwise, when they get to the long start-finish straight Dovizioso's powerful Ducati will come flying past again.

We later found out that Rossi really enjoyed the fight with Dovizioso:

In the end, though, Rossi does get the gap he needs, and stays ahead.

@ValeYellow46
Yesterday's great battle with Andrea Dovizioso!

↩   🔁 44   ⭐ 21   •••

cooked used up and without much grip left

LAP 8 For the last few laps, Marc has been half a second faster than Rossi. Now, though, Rossi catches up a tenth-of-a-second between turns 2 and 10.

It's not ideal — but they're on a bendy part of the circuit, where we expect Rossi's Yamaha to be fast. Our bike is better in different parts of the track, where there's a bend followed by a chance to accelerate hard. A moment later, the race commentary had us all smiling:

> "That Repsol Honda is [famous] for its 'get out of the corner and squirt' speed."

LAP 11 Marc is still 3 seconds ahead. Things are looking good — but we've all seen Rossi close bigger gaps than this one at the end of a race. The victory isn't safe yet!

squirt bike-racer slang for accelerating very quickly and suddenly

TYRE TROUBLE
FOR THE DOCTOR

At some circuits, with fewer than ten laps to race it's pretty clear who will win. That's not necessarily true here!

The reason is that this Austin circuit wears out front tyres more quickly than just about anywhere else. If a rider brakes and corners fiercely in the early part of the race, he'll be able to keep up for a while. Then the bike's front tyre starts to lose grip — and as the commentator says:

"There's nothing you can do on a motorbike when it starts washing out every time you [turn into a corner]."

Last year, Rossi had big problems towards the end of the race. His front tyre wore out, and he was a sitting duck for riders behind. In the end he only managed to finish eighth.

washing out sideways slide of the bike's front wheel, caused by loss of grip from the front tyre

LAP 13 Rossi starts to drop back. It's not that Marc's going faster — it's just that Rossi can't keep up the pace. He's falling back into the clutches of Dovizioso:

Race commentary: "Valentino Rossi is in all sorts of trouble here. The two Ducatis are going to swamp him towards the end."

Meanwhile, Marc's lead increases to 3.4 seconds:

Race commentary: "Marc Marquez looks at the moment like he's going to take his third Grand Prix of the Americas."

LAP 15 Things get even better for Marc. Dovizioso overtakes Rossi, who has the other Ducati bike behind him. Rossi is now the filling in a Ducati sandwich.

Marc, meanwhile, now has a lead of 4.5 seconds.

LAST LAPS

You can never relax in motorbike racing. Disaster can always strike. What if Marc sees the same warning light as during qualifying, for example?*

*He'd probably keep riding until the engine blew up or he crossed the line!

Barring disaster, though, it does look like Marc is going to win this race. He's managed his tyres brilliantly, pulling away from Rossi at just the perfect moment. We can start to enjoy watching the race a bit more, now that Marc looks safe in first place!

LAP 18 There seem to be two fights going on, for second and fourth. Rossi is battling Dovizioso for second. Behind them, the second Ducati bike is in fourth — until Lorenzo slices past!

Race commentary: "Absolute poetry from Jorge — totally calculated, wonderfully executed."

We'd forgotten Lorenzo, who's been riding around basically on his own for ages. Apparently he's been saving the grip on his tyres, and is now on a charge.

on a charge riding fast enough to catch riders ahead very quickly

LAP 19 You can see in the slow-motion replays that Rossi's tyres are almost shredded. He's obviously struggling, and it looks impossible for him to catch Dovizioso and grab second.

FINAL LAP No one wants to risk crashing and coming nowhere, after riding so hard all weekend. Marc crosses the line in first, Dovizioso is second, Rossi third, and Lorenzo fourth.

GRAND PRIX
OF THE
AMERICAS
Circuit of the Americas 2015

@marcmarquez93
First victory of the year! #AmericasGP

You can see in the photo how happy Marc was. Marc is now only 5 points behind Rossi in the riders' World Championship. And as you get 25, 20 and 16 points for first, second and third in each race, he can catch that up really quickly.

Even so, it does look like it's going to be a tight season!*

*The winner of the 2015 season is revealed on page 32.

SO YOU WANT TO RACE IN MOTOGP?

When you watch a MotoGP race, it's hard not to dream of being on the bike yourself. Getting into MotoGP is very competitive, of course — but some people do make it! Marc's story is a good example of how it can happen:

START YOUNG

It's not exactly true to say that Marc grew up on a motorbike — but he did get his first one before he started school!

"I really loved bikes, and I got my first one when I was only four, as a present from my parents."

Even today he says:

"The thing I have that is the most valuable to me is my first ever bike"!

RIDE ROAD AND OFF-ROAD

Marc began motorcycling on an off-road bike. When he was eight years old, he started racing in the Catalonian Championship. (Catalonia is the region in Spain where Marc lives.) Later he began racing on the road as well, but even today Marc still uses off-road riding to improve his riding skills.

MAKE YOUR WAY THROUGH THE CLASSES

Marc began his career racing 125cc bikes in local competitions, then moved to bigger leagues. He won the World 125cc Championship in 2010 (shown above), then began to race on 600cc bikes in Moto2. He won the Moto2 World Championship in 2012, and moved to MotoGP in 2013.

Marc's rise through the classes has been amazing — it takes most riders much longer to get a chance in MotoGP. But Marc's kid brother Alex seems to be following the same path: he won the Moto3 title, for 250cc bikes, in 2014, and moved into Moto2 for 2015.

MORE TOP RIDERS

Marc Marquez raced in the 2015 Riders' Championship alongside some great bike racers, whose bios are featured in this book. Here are a few more famous names from the world of motorcycle racing:

RIDER BIO

NAME: Giacomo Agostini **NATIONALITY:** Italian **BORN:** 1942

The first ever superstar bike racer, Agostini is often said to be the best rider ever. He won 15 World Championships in the 350cc and 500cc classes — including both titles every year between 1968 and 1972.

RIDER BIO

NAME: Wayne Rainey **NATIONALITY:** US **BORN:** 1960

Rainey won three World Championships in a row (1990—92) during the "Golden Age" of motorbike racing. At that time, the 500cc bikes were so powerful and hard to control that they regularly spat their riders off.

RIDER BIO

NAME: Barry Sheene **NATIONALITY:** British **LIVED:** 1950—2003

500cc World Champion in 1976 and 1977, Sheene was a hero to many bike-racing fans. He was almost as famous for his crashes as his victories: in 1982 he was on course for a third world title, until a terrible accident in practice broke both his legs.

RIDER BIO

NAME: Casey Stoner **NATIONALITY:** Australian **BORN:** 1985

Stoner seems able to ride almost any bike to victory. He won world titles in 2007, on a hard-to-control Ducati, and 2011, on a smooth-as-silk Honda. Stoner retired from MotoGP in 2012, but rumours persist of a comeback.

RIDER BIO

NAME: Joey Dunlop **NATIONALITY:** Northern Irish **LIVED:** 1952—2000

Though not a MotoGP star, Dunlop was one of the greatest road racers ever. Winner of 26 Isle of Man TT races and 24 Ulster Grand Prix, Dunlop was Formula One TT World Champion five times. Tragically, he died after crashing in a race in Estonia.

MotoGP races are held in Asia, Australia, Europe, the Middle East, and North and South America. Some racetracks, though, are special to the fans and the drivers:

TT ASSEN, ASSEN, NETHERLANDS

Bikers know Assen simply as "The Cathedral". Every year, tens of thousands flock here from all over the world to watch the action. The track started life in 1949, when it followed public roads through the local villages. In 1954 it was turned into a full-time race circuit.

WATCH OUT FOR: if you're actually at Assen on the Thursday or Friday, you may be able to arrange a walk around the circuit. Once the action gets going, the final chicane is a good place to watch the racing.

CZECH REPUBLIC GRAND PRIX, BRNO

If you like a crowd, head for Brno during the MotoGP weekend. Over quarter of a million people regularly turn up to watch the racing, which is usually very close. The atmospheric location, surrounded by forest, makes the racing almost as much fun to see on TV.

WATCH OUT FOR: the four turns known together as Stadion (Stadium). This banked area is where many of the race's overtakes happen.

ITALIAN GRAND PRIX, MUGELLO

Valentino Rossi has won nine times (and counting) at Mugello, and considers it his home race. The organisers now expect a crowd invasion of the start-finish straight whenever Rossi finishes a race there — whether he wins or not.

WATCH OUT FOR: the mixture of fast and slow corners, off-camber turns and long straights, which make Mugello one of the most difficult circuits for the racers.

AUSTRALIAN GRAND PRIX, PHILLIP ISLAND

This must be the world's most spectacular racetrack. The circuit swoops and rises, twists and turns, while in the background waves crash in from the Southern Ocean. Sometimes it looks as though overcooking a bend could pitch you straight into the sea!

WATCH OUT FOR: the top speeds set on the start-finish straight, where the riders regularly reach over 330 kph.

---

off-camber a road surface that tilts away from the direction of the corner

GLOSSARY

250cc/500cc, etc — The "cc" stands for cylinder capacity of the motorbike engine. The higher the number, the bigger and more powerful the engine.

chicane — Bends added to a track so that the racers have to slow down to steer through safely.

circuit — A racetrack or route that starts and finishes at the same place.

data — Statistics and facts that are recorded for analysis.

footpeg — The part of a motorbike where the rider rests his foot/feet.

free-practice session (FP) — The opportunity for competitors to try out their motorbike on the circuit prior to a race.

grid — The pattern of lines that marks the start on a motor racing track.

lap — One circuit of a racetrack.

MotoGP — Motorbike Grand Prix, the highest level of competition in motorbike track racing. MotoGP riders race on 1,000cc bikes. (Moto2 riders race 600cc bikes, and Moto3 riders use 250cc bikes.

pit — An area at the side of a racetrack where racing bikes or cars are serviced or refuelled by the pit crew, a team of race engineers.

pit lane — A side road parallel to the racetrack, which leads in and out of the pit.

pole-sitter — The racer who begins the race from the front of the starting grid, which is known as "pole position".

qualifying — Timed laps done before a race, which decide who gets the best positions on the grid.

race commentary — The spoken account of the race that is broadcast to the spectators (at home or at the racetrack) describing a race as it happens.

satellite (bike team) — A smaller racing team with a lower budget that is assisted by a main bike manufacturer's team.

sitting duck — Someone who it is easy for a rival or enemy to attack.

slogan — A phrase, often used in advertising.

suspension — Shock absorbers on a motorbike that absorb bumps in the road.

time sheet — Here, a printed piece of paper used to record how fast each rider completes each lap or each level of the competition.

INDEX

The winner of the 2015 MotoGP season was Jorge Lorenzo for the Movistar Yamaha team.